PSALMS
OF
Thanksgivnig

A WORSHIP THROUGH THE WORD STUDY JOURNAL

by
CARI BARNEY

BRAND NEW HOPE

AT BRAND NEW HOPE OUR MISSION IS TO ENCOURAGE AND EQUIP WOMEN TO FIND BRAND NEW HOPE IN CHRIST AND HIS WORD

Our prayer is to help you move beyond devotionals and study scripture more in depth. We want you to find time daily in your busy schedule to hunger for God's Word and read and understand it more fully so you can grow in your relationship with Him. Our Bible Study Method; WORSHIP Through The Word, and our Bible Study Journals will teach you how to study the Word of God in depth in as little as 15 minutes a day. Allow you to understand scripture more fully. Grow closer in your relationship with God, and build a solid foundation for studying any part of the Bible.

Are you ready? Let's dive in!

CONTENTS

Welcome

Every Thanksgiving one of my favorite things to do is to reminisce over the past year and give thanks to God for everything he has done. I praise him for his goodness, I praise him for loved one's near and far, and I praise him even for the heartache and sorrow.

For me, Thanksgiving is my favorite holiday because it is an opportunity to count my blessings, and cultivate a heart of gratitude. It can be easy to look at Thanksgiving as a prelude to the Christmas season, however, I want to challenge you through this Bible Study to embrace Thanksgiving as a moment to pause and thank our Heavenly Father for who he is, and what he has done in your life.

Each day before reading the scripture(s) pray and ask God to help you cultivate a heart of Thanksgiving and praise. Allow him to speak to you through His Word, and take time to listen to the promptings of the Holy Spirit.

Take your time as you read each scripture passage and allow it to sink into your mind and heart. Look at each scripture reading and the promptings used in the WORSHIP Through The Word study method as an opportunity to dig into scripture like you are mining for buried treasure.

Carve out 15-30 minutes per day to complete this study and prepare your space by having your resources ready. Block out any distractions, and play some worship music in the background to usher in the presence of the Holy Spirit.

Are you ready? Let's begin!

Blessings,

Cari Barney

Founder: Brand New Hope

Join Us

ON LINE

WWW.BRANDNEWHOPE.NET

SHOP

WWW.BRANDNEWHOPE.NET/SHOP

FACEBOOK

FACEBOOK.COM/BRANDNEWHOPE

INSTAGRAM

INSTAGRAM.COM/BRANDNEWHOPE_

CONTACT US

INFO@BRANDNEWHOPE.NET

CONNECT

#BRANDNEWHOPE

Worship

GETTING STARTED

WORSHIP is an acronym for the Bible study method that we will use that will allow you to spend more time intentionally studying the Word of God with open hearts and minds. Spending time in reading and meditating on Scripture is the ultimate form of worship because the Word of God is His love letter to you! There are layers of meaning in the pages of scripture that will unfold for you as you spend more time in the Bible. By using the WORSHIP bible study method you will be nourished through the living and active Word, You will begin to crave the time you spend in scripture during your WORSHIP time. Guard this time, and prepare your heart and mind through prayer and praise before beginning. Ask the Holy Spirit to speak to you through the Scripture. Play some praise and worship music in the background to usher in the presence of the Holy Spirit. There are a few tools that you will need, but most are free or you already have them on hand!

Below you will find a list of my favorite resources.

TOOLS + RESOURCES

- Study Bible (I prefer the ESV Study Bible (App or Physical Bible)
- Pens
- Highlighters or Colored Pens
- Printable WORSHIP Study Guide
- Blue Letter Bible (App or Website)
- Bible Hub (App or Website)
- YouVersion Bible (App)

Worship

THE METHOD

————————

W

Write the verse or passage that you are studying. Circle any words that stand out to you or that you want to understand better. Highlight transition words (And, Therefore, Because etc.). Highlight any references to God, Jesus, or the Holy Spirit. Highlight any promises of God. Highlight any commands. Finally highlight any sins to avoid, or behavior to follow.

O

Observe the surrounding verses for contextual clues. Write down who wrote the passage, or who is the passage about. What is happening in the passage? When in the context of scripture is the passage taking place? What is the main event or circumstance of the passage? Where is the passage taking place? Why is the event or circumstance happening in the passage?

R

Research the words in the passage or verse that you circled by using the Blue Letter Bible Interlinear Concordance in the original Greek or Hebrew language. Write down the definition of the words. Write down any cross references pertaining to the passage and read them. Make note of any commentary that stands out to you using your Study Bible notes or Blue Letter Bible or Bible Hub.

S

Summarize your findings. How does the original language of the words that you researched bring new meaning to the passage? How does the cross referenced verses relate to one another and the overall message of redemption found in the Bible. What does this verse or passage teach you about God/Jesus/Holy Spirit and your relationship with Him? What does this passage or verse teach you about yourself and others?

H

How is the Holy Spirit speaking to you through this verse or passage of scripture? Pray and ask the Holy Spirit to open your heart and mind. Time yourself for one minute and listen to what the Holy Spirit is saying to you. Write down what you hear.

I

Internalize and Apply the passage or verse to you and your walk with the Lord. Is there anything that you are convicted of? Are there any behaviors or thinking that you need to change? Are there any beliefs that are untrue that you need to transform with the truth of God's Word? Are there any desires that need to be changed in your heart? Is there any actions that God wants you to take? Write these things down.

P

Pray through the verse or passage . Thank the Lord for his truths written in the Word and for speaking to your heart and mind. Confess any sins revealed to you through the scripture and ask the Lord to help you to change. Write down your prayer.

Recipe

NANA'S APPLE PIE

Ingredients

- 5 to 7 Medium Tart Apples
- 3/4 to 1 Cup Sugar
- 2 Tablespoons Flour
- Dash of Salt
- 2 Teaspoons Cinnamon
- 2 Tablespoons Butter or Margarine
- 1 Package Pillsbury Pie Crust

This classic Thanksgiving recipe is a favorite for our family every year. This recipe is especially precious because my Nana would use Papa's fresh apples from his apple tree. After moving to the south from western New York, Papa's apples are greatly missed. I pray you enjoy this recipe and make it a tradition on your Thanksgiving table each year!

Directions

- Preheat oven to 400 degrees Fahrenheit
- Lightly spray a 9 inch pie pan with cooking spray
- Line the pie pan with 1 package of Pillsbury pie dough.
- Pare apples and slice thin and pour into pie pan
- In a small bowl mix sugar, salt, flour, cinnamon, nutmeg, and sprinkle evenly on top of the apples
- Dot apples with butter
- Cut top pie crust into even strips using a pizza cutter
- Overlap pie crust strips into a lattice on top of the apples
- Pinch edges of bottom and top of pie crust to join
- Sprinkle top pie crust with sugar if desired
- Bake at 400 degrees Fahrenheit for 50 minutes or until crust is golden brown

PSALMS

OF

Thanksgiving

LET'S BEGIN

Reading Plan

WEEK 1

DAY 1 - Give Thanks For Family
READ: Psalm 106: 47-48, 1 Chronicles 16:34-36
WORSHIP: Psalm 106:47

DAY 2 - Give Thanks For All God Has Done
READ: Psalm 9:1-2, Psalm 26:7, Psalm 40:5, Psalm 96: 2-4
WORSHIP: Psalm 9:1-2

DAY 3 - Give Thanks For Deliverance
READ: Psalm 69:30-36
WORSHIP: Psalm 69:33

DAY 4 - Give Thanks To God For Being Our Shepherd
READ: Psalm 95:1-11
WORSHIP: Psalm 95:7-8

DAY 5 - Give Thanks For God's Faithfulness
READ: Psalm 100:1-5
WORSHIP: Psalm 100:5

DAY 6 - Give Thanks For God's Protection
READ: Psalm 118:1-9
WORSHIP: Psalm 118:5-6

DAY 7 - Give Thanks To God For His Salvation
READ: Psalm 118:19-26
WORSHIP: Psalm 118:24

WEEK 2

DAY 1 - Give Thanks For Children
READ: Psalm 127:3-5, Deuteronomy 28:4-6
WORSHIP: Psalm 127:3

DAY 2 - Give Thanks For Siblings
READ: Psalm 133:1-3, Genesis 13:8, Hebrews 13:1
WORSHIP: Psalm 133:1

DAY 3 - Give Thanks To God For Protecting Widows And Orphans
READ: Psalm 68:3-6, Deuteronomy 10:18, Psalm 32:11
WORSHIP: Psalm 68:5

DAY 4 - Give Thanks To God For A Legacy of Faith
READ: Psalm 145:1-7
WORSHIP: Psalm 145:4

DAY 5 - Give Thanks for God's Goodness
READ: Psalm 145:8-13
WORSHIP: Psalm 145:8-9

DAY 6 - Give Thanks for God's Generosity
READ: Psalm 145:14-20, Psalm 104:27-28
WORSHIP: Psalm 145:15-16

DAY 7: Give Thanks for God's Provision Of Food
READ: Psalm 107:8-9, Psalm 34:10, Psalm 146:7, Luke 1:53
WORSHIP: Psalm 107:9

Reading Plan

WEEK 3

DAY 1 - Give Thanks To God For His Righteousness
READ: Psalm 106:1-3, 1 John 2:28-29, 1 John 3:7
WORSHIP: 1 John 2:29

DAY 2 - Give Thanks To God For Our Cities
READ: Psalm 107:1-7, Psalm 107:36
WORSHIP: Psalm 107:7

DAY 3 - Give Thanks To God For His Protection
READ: Psalm 28:6-9, Psalm 3:3-4, Psalm 11:1
WORSHIP: Psalm 28:7

DAY 4 - Give Thanks To God For His Many Benefits
READ: Psalm 116:12-19
WORSHIP: Psalm 116:17

DAY 5 - Give Thanks To God For Loving Us Although We Are Sinners
READ: Psalm 117:1-2, Psalm 103:11-16
WORSHIP: Psalm 103:12

DAY 6 - Give Thanks To God For Knowing Us Intimately
READ: Psalm 139:1-6
WORSHIP: Psalm 139:1

DAY 7 - Give Thanks To God For His Word
READ: Psalm 119:1-8
WORSHIP: Psalm 119:7

WEEK 4

DAY 1 - Give Thanks To God For Being The One True God
READ: Psalm 136:1-9
WORSHIP: Psalm 136:2

DAY 2 - Give Thanks To God For Remembering Us In Our Time Of Need
READ: Psalm 136:23-26
WORSHIP: Psalm 136:23

DAY 3 - Give Thanks To God For Ordering Our Steps
READ: Psalm 50:14-15; 23
WORSHIP: Psalm 50:23

DAY 4 - Give Thanks To God For Rest
READ: Psalm 92:1-5
WORSHIP: Psalm 92:4

DAY 5 - Give Thanks To God For His Holiness
READ: Psalm Psalm 96:1-13
WORSHIP: Psalm 96:9

DAY 6 - Give Thanks To God For His Mercy
READ: Psalm 103:1-9
WORSHIP: Psalm 103:8

DAY 7: Give Thanks To God For His Continuous Wondrous Works
READ: Psalm 105:1-5
WORSHIP: Psalm 105:4

Let us come into his presence with thanksgiving Let us make a joyful noise to him with songs of praise!

PSALM 95:2

READ
Psalm 106:47-48, 1 Chronicles 16:34-36

WORSHIP
Psalm 106:47

Psalm 106:47–48

47 Save us, O LORD our God,
and gather us from among the nations,
that we may give thanks to your holy name
and glory in your praise.
48 Blessed be the LORD, the God of Israel,
from everlasting to everlasting!
And let all the people say, "Amen!"
Praise the LORD!

1 Chronicles 16:34–36

34 Oh give thanks to the LORD, for he is good;
for his steadfast love endures forever!
35 Say also:
"Save us, O God of our salvation,
and gather and deliver us from among the nations,
that we may give thanks to your holy name
and glory in your praise.
36 Blessed be the LORD, the God of Israel,
from everlasting to everlasting!"
Then all the people said, "Amen!" and praised the LORD.

W WRITE THE VERSE - CIRCLE WORDS TO LOOK UP - HIGHLIGHT

_____

_____

_____

_____

_____

_____

_____

O OBSERVE - READ SURROUNDING VERSES - WHO, WHAT, WHEN, WHERE, HOW, WHY

_____

_____

_____

_____

_____

_____

_____

R RESEARCH - LOOK UP WORDS - CROSS REFERENCES - COMMENTARY

_____

_____

_____

_____

_____

_____

_____

S SUMMARY - SUMMARIZE YOUR FINDINGS-WHAT DOES THE PASSAGE TEACH YOU ABOUT YOUR RELATIONSHIP WITH GOD AND OTHERS

H HOLY SPIRIT - PRAY AND ASK THE HOLY SPIRIT TO SPEAK TO YOU THROUGH THE PASSAGE - WRITE DOWN WHAT YOU HEAR

I INTERNALIZE AND APPLY - HOW DOES THE PASSAGE RELATE TO YOU AND YOUR WALK WITH THE LORD

P PRAY - PRAY THROUGH THE VERSE OR PASSAGE -THANK THE LORD FOR HIS TRUTHS WRITTEN IN THE WORD

READ
Psalm 9:1-2, Psalm 26:7, Psalm 40:5, Psalm 96:2-4

WORSHIP
Psalm 9:1-2

———————

Psalm 9:1–2

1 I will give thanks to the LORD with my whole heart;
I will recount all of your wonderful deeds.
2 I will be glad and exult in you;
I will sing praise to your name, O Most High.

Psalm 26:7

7 proclaiming thanksgiving aloud,
and telling all your wondrous deeds.

Psalm 40:5

5 You have multiplied, O **LORD** my God,
your wondrous deeds and your thoughts toward us;
none can compare with you!
I will proclaim and tell of them,
yet they are more than can be told.

Psalm 96:2-4

2 Sing to the LORD, bless his name;
tell of his salvation from day to day.
3 Declare his glory among the nations,
his marvelous works among all the peoples!
4 For great is the LORD, and greatly to be praised;
he is to be feared above all gods.

Worship Through The Word

W   **WRITE THE VERSE** - CIRCLE WORDS TO LOOK UP - HIGHLIGHT

_____

_____

_____

_____

_____

_____

_____

_____

O   **OBSERVE** - READ SURROUNDING VERSES - WHO, WHAT, WHEN, WHERE, HOW, WHY

_____

_____

_____

_____

_____

_____

_____

_____

R   **RESEARCH** - LOOK UP WORDS - CROSS REFERENCES - COMMENTARY

_____

_____

_____

_____

_____

_____

_____

_____

S SUMMARY - SUMMARIZE YOUR FINDINGS-WHAT DOES THE PASSAGE TEACH YOU ABOUT YOUR RELATIONSHIP WITH GOD AND OTHERS

H HOLY SPIRIT - PRAY AND ASK THE HOLY SPIRIT TO SPEAK TO YOU THROUGH THE PASSAGE - WRITE DOWN WHAT YOU HEAR

I INTERNALIZE AND APPLY - HOW DOES THE PASSAGE RELATE TO YOU AND YOUR WALK WITH THE LORD

P PRAY - PRAY THROUGH THE VERSE OR PASSAGE -THANK THE LORD FOR HIS TRUTHS WRITTEN IN THE WORD

READ

Psalm 69:30-36

WORSHIP

Psalm 69:33

Psalm 69:30-36

30 I will praise the name of God with a song;

I will magnify him with thanksgiving.

31 This will please the LORD more than an ox

or a bull with horns and hoofs.

32 When the humble see it they will be glad;

you who seek God, let your hearts revive.

33 For the LORD hears the needy

and does not despise his own people who are prisoners.

34 Let heaven and earth praise him,

the seas and everything that moves in them.

35 For God will save Zion

and build up the cities of Judah,

and people shall dwell there and possess it;

36 the offspring of his servants shall inherit it,

and those who love his name shall dwell in it.

Worship Through The Word

W WRITE THE VERSE - CIRCLE WORDS TO LOOK UP - HIGHLIGHT

_____

_____

_____

_____

_____

_____

_____

_____

O OBSERVE - READ SURROUNDING VERSES - WHO, WHAT, WHEN, WHERE, HOW, WHY

_____

_____

_____

_____

_____

_____

_____

_____

_____

R RESEARCH - LOOK UP WORDS - CROSS REFERENCES - COMMENTARY

_____

_____

_____

_____

_____

_____

_____

_____

S SUMMARY - SUMMARIZE YOUR FINDINGS-WHAT DOES THE PASSAGE TEACH YOU ABOUT YOUR RELATIONSHIP WITH GOD AND OTHERS

H HOLY SPIRIT - PRAY AND ASK THE HOLY SPIRIT TO SPEAK TO YOU THROUGH THE PASSAGE - WRITE DOWN WHAT YOU HEAR

I INTERNALIZE AND APPLY - HOW DOES THE PASSAGE RELATE TO YOU AND YOUR WALK WITH THE LORD

P PRAY - PRAY THROUGH THE VERSE OR PASSAGE -THANK THE LORD FOR HIS TRUTHS WRITTEN IN THE WORD

READ
Psalm 95:1-11

WORSHIP
Psalm 95:7-8

———————

Psalm 95:1-11

1 Oh come, let us sing to the LORD;

let us make a joyful noise to the rock of our salvation!

2 Let us come into his presence with thanksgiving;

let us make a joyful noise to him with songs of praise!

3 For the LORD is a great God,

and a great King above all gods.

4 In his hand are the depths of the earth;

the heights of the mountains are his also.

5 The sea is his, for he made it,

and his hands formed the dry land.

6 Oh come, let us worship and bow down;

let us kneel before the LORD, our Maker!

7 For he is our God,

and we are the people of his pasture,

and the sheep of his hand.

Today, if you hear his voice,

8 do not harden your hearts, as at Meribah,

as on the day at Massah in the wilderness,

9 when your fathers put me to the test

and put me to the proof, though they had seen my work.

10 For forty years I loathed that generation

and said, "They are a people who go astray in their heart,

and they have not known my ways."

11 Therefore I swore in my wrath,

"They shall not enter my rest."

Worship Through The Word

W **WRITE THE VERSE** - CIRCLE WORDS TO LOOK UP - HIGHLIGHT

_____

_____

_____

_____

_____

_____

_____

O **OBSERVE** - READ SURROUNDING VERSES - WHO, WHAT, WHEN, WHERE, HOW, WHY

_____

_____

_____

_____

_____

_____

_____

_____

_____

R **RESEARCH** - LOOK UP WORDS - CROSS REFERENCES - COMMENTARY

_____

_____

_____

_____

_____

_____

_____

_____

S SUMMARY - SUMMARIZE YOUR FINDINGS-WHAT DOES THE PASSAGE TEACH YOU ABOUT YOUR RELATIONSHIP WITH GOD AND OTHERS

H HOLY SPIRIT - PRAY AND ASK THE HOLY SPIRIT TO SPEAK TO YOU THROUGH THE PASSAGE - WRITE DOWN WHAT YOU HEAR

I INTERNALIZE AND APPLY - HOW DOES THE PASSAGE RELATE TO YOU AND YOUR WALK WITH THE LORD

P PRAY - PRAY THROUGH THE VERSE OR PASSAGE -THANK THE LORD FOR HIS TRUTHS WRITTEN IN THE WORD

READ
Psalm 100:1-5

WORSHIP
Psalm 100:5

_____

Psalm 100:1-5

1 Make a joyful noise to the LORD, all the earth!

2 Serve the LORD with gladness!

Come into his presence with singing!

3 Know that the LORD, he is God!

It is he who made us, and we are his;

we are his people, and the sheep of his pasture.

4 Enter his gates with thanksgiving,

and his courts with praise!

Give thanks to him; bless his name!

5 For the LORD is good;

his steadfast love endures forever,

and his faithfulness to all generations.

Worship Through The Word

W | **WRITE THE VERSE** - CIRCLE WORDS TO LOOK UP - HIGHLIGHT

_____
_____
_____
_____
_____
_____
_____

O | **OBSERVE** - READ SURROUNDING VERSES - WHO, WHAT, WHEN, WHERE, HOW, WHY

_____
_____
_____
_____
_____
_____
_____
_____

R | **RESEARCH** - LOOK UP WORDS - CROSS REFERENCES - COMMENTARY

_____
_____
_____
_____
_____
_____
_____
_____

S **SUMMARY** - SUMMARIZE YOUR FINDINGS-WHAT DOES THE PASSAGE TEACH YOU ABOUT YOUR RELATIONSHIP WITH GOD AND OTHERS

H **HOLY SPIRIT -** PRAY AND ASK THE HOLY SPIRIT TO SPEAK TO YOU THROUGH THE PASSAGE - WRITE DOWN WHAT YOU HEAR

I **INTERNALIZE AND APPLY** - HOW DOES THE PASSAGE RELATE TO YOU AND YOUR WALK WITH THE LORD

P **PRAY** - PRAY THROUGH THE VERSE OR PASSAGE -THANK THE LORD FOR HIS TRUTHS WRITTEN IN THE WORD

READ
Psalm 118:1-9

WORSHIP
Psalm 118:5-6

Psalm 118:1-9

1 Oh give thanks to the LORD, for he is good;
for his steadfast love endures forever!
2 Let Israel say,
"His steadfast love endures forever."
3 Let the house of Aaron say,
"His steadfast love endures forever."
4 Let those who fear the LORD say,
"His steadfast love endures forever."
5 Out of my distress I called on the LORD;
the LORD answered me and set me free.
6 The LORD is on my side; I will not fear.
What can man do to me?
7 The LORD is on my side as my helper;
I shall look in triumph on those who hate me.
8 It is better to take refuge in the LORD
than to trust in man.
9 It is better to take refuge in the LORD
than to trust in princes.

W WRITE THE VERSE - CIRCLE WORDS TO LOOK UP - HIGHLIGHT

_____

_____

_____

_____

_____

_____

_____

O OBSERVE - READ SURROUNDING VERSES - WHO, WHAT, WHEN, WHERE, HOW, WHY

_____

_____

_____

_____

_____

_____

_____

_____

R RESEARCH - LOOK UP WORDS - CROSS REFERENCES - COMMENTARY

_____

_____

_____

_____

_____

_____

_____

S SUMMARY - SUMMARIZE YOUR FINDINGS-WHAT DOES THE PASSAGE TEACH YOU ABOUT YOUR RELATIONSHIP WITH GOD AND OTHERS

H HOLY SPIRIT - PRAY AND ASK THE HOLY SPIRIT TO SPEAK TO YOU THROUGH THE PASSAGE - WRITE DOWN WHAT YOU HEAR

I INTERNALIZE AND APPLY - HOW DOES THE PASSAGE RELATE TO YOU AND YOUR WALK WITH THE LORD

P PRAY - PRAY THROUGH THE VERSE OR PASSAGE -THANK THE LORD FOR HIS TRUTHS WRITTEN IN THE WORD

———————————

Psalm 118:19-26

19 Open to me the gates of righteousness,
that I may enter through them
and give thanks to the LORD.
20 This is the gate of the LORD;
the righteous shall enter through it.
21 I thank you that you have answered me
and have become my salvation.
22 The stone that the builders rejected
has become the cornerstone.
23 This is the LORD's doing;
it is marvelous in our eyes.
24 This is the day that the LORD has made;
let us rejoice and be glad in it.
25 Save us, we pray, O LORD!
O LORD, we pray, give us success!
26 Blessed is he who comes in the name of the LORD!
We bless you from the house of the LORD.

Worship Through The Word

W   **WRITE THE VERSE** - CIRCLE WORDS TO LOOK UP - HIGHLIGHT

O   **OBSERVE** - READ SURROUNDING VERSES - WHO, WHAT, WHEN, WHERE, HOW, WHY

R   **RESEARCH** - LOOK UP WORDS - CROSS REFERENCES - COMMENTARY

S **SUMMARY** - SUMMARIZE YOUR FINDINGS-WHAT DOES THE PASSAGE TEACH YOU ABOUT YOUR RELATIONSHIP WITH GOD AND OTHERS

H **HOLY SPIRIT -** PRAY AND ASK THE HOLY SPIRIT TO SPEAK TO YOU THROUGH THE PASSAGE - WRITE DOWN WHAT YOU HEAR

I **INTERNALIZE AND APPLY** - HOW DOES THE PASSAGE RELATE TO YOU AND YOUR WALK WITH THE LORD

P **PRAY** - PRAY THROUGH THE VERSE OR PASSAGE -THANK THE LORD FOR HIS TRUTHS WRITTEN IN THE WORD

Behold, how good and pleasant it is when brothers dwell in unity!

PSALM 133:1

READ
Psalm 127:3-5, Deuteronomy 28:4-6

WORSHIP
Psalm 127:3

Psalm 127:305

3 Behold, children are a heritage from the LORD,
the fruit of the womb a reward.
4 Like arrows in the hand of a warrior
are the children of one's youth.
5 Blessed is the man
who fills his quiver with them!
He shall not be put to shame
when he speaks with his enemies in the gate.

Deuteronomy 28:4-6

4 Blessed shall be the fruit of your womb
and the fruit of your ground
and the fruit of your cattle,
the increase of your herds and the young of your flock.
5 Blessed shall be your basket
and your kneading bowl.
6 Blessed shall you be when you come in,
and blessed shall you be when you go out.

Worship Through The Word

W **WRITE THE VERSE** - CIRCLE WORDS TO LOOK UP - HIGHLIGHT

_____
_____
_____
_____
_____
_____
_____

O **OBSERVE** - READ SURROUNDING VERSES - WHO, WHAT, WHEN, WHERE, HOW, WHY

_____
_____
_____
_____
_____
_____
_____
_____

R **RESEARCH** - LOOK UP WORDS - CROSS REFERENCES - COMMENTARY

_____
_____
_____
_____
_____
_____

S **SUMMARY** - SUMMARIZE YOUR FINDINGS-WHAT DOES THE PASSAGE TEACH YOU ABOUT YOUR RELATIONSHIP WITH GOD AND OTHERS

H **HOLY SPIRIT -** PRAY AND ASK THE HOLY SPIRIT TO SPEAK TO YOU THROUGH THE PASSAGE - WRITE DOWN WHAT YOU HEAR

I **INTERNALIZE AND APPLY** - HOW DOES THE PASSAGE RELATE TO YOU AND YOUR WALK WITH THE LORD

P **PRAY** - PRAY THROUGH THE VERSE OR PASSAGE -THANK THE LORD FOR HIS TRUTHS WRITTEN IN THE WORD

READ

Psalm 133:1-3, Genesis 13:8, Hebrews 13:1

WORSHIP

Psalm 133:1

Psalm 133:1-3

Behold, how good and pleasant it is
when brothers dwell in unity!
2 It is like the precious oil on the head,
running down on the beard,
on the beard of Aaron,
running down on the collar of his robes!
3 It is like the dew of Hermon,
which falls on the mountains of Zion!
For there the LORD has commanded the blessing,
life forevermore.

Genesis 13:8

8 Then Abram said to Lot,
"Let there be no strife between you and me,
and between your herdsmen and my herdsmen,
for we are kinsmen.

Hebrews 13:1

1 Let brotherly love continue.

Worship Through The Word

W   **WRITE THE VERSE** - CIRCLE WORDS TO LOOK UP - HIGHLIGHT

_____

_____

_____

_____

_____

_____

_____

O   **OBSERVE** - READ SURROUNDING VERSES - WHO, WHAT, WHEN, WHERE, HOW, WHY

_____

_____

_____

_____

_____

_____

_____

R   **RESEARCH** - LOOK UP WORDS - CROSS REFERENCES - COMMENTARY

_____

_____

_____

_____

_____

_____

_____

S SUMMARY - SUMMARIZE YOUR FINDINGS-WHAT DOES THE PASSAGE TEACH YOU ABOUT YOUR RELATIONSHIP WITH GOD AND OTHERS

H HOLY SPIRIT - PRAY AND ASK THE HOLY SPIRIT TO SPEAK TO YOU THROUGH THE PASSAGE - WRITE DOWN WHAT YOU HEAR

I INTERNALIZE AND APPLY - HOW DOES THE PASSAGE RELATE TO YOU AND YOUR WALK WITH THE LORD

P PRAY - PRAY THROUGH THE VERSE OR PASSAGE -THANK THE LORD FOR HIS TRUTHS WRITTEN IN THE WORD

READ
Psalm 68:3-6, Deuteronomy 10:18, Psalm 32:11

WORSHIP
Psalm 68:5

Psalm 68:3-6

3 But the righteous shall be glad;
they shall exult before God;
they shall be jubilant with joy!
4 Sing to God, sing praises to his name;
lift up a song to him who rides through the deserts;
his name is the LORD;
exult before him!
5 Father of the fatherless and protector of widows
is God in his holy habitation.
6 God settles the solitary in a home;
he leads out the prisoners to prosperity,
but the rebellious dwell in a parched land.

Deuteronomy 10:18

18 He executes justice for the fatherless and the widow,
and loves the sojourner,
giving him food and clothing.

Psalm 32:11

11 Be glad in the LORD, and rejoice, O righteous,
and shout for joy, all you upright in heart!

Worship Through The Word

W **WRITE THE VERSE** - CIRCLE WORDS TO LOOK UP - HIGHLIGHT

O **OBSERVE** - READ SURROUNDING VERSES - WHO, WHAT, WHEN, WHERE, HOW, WHY

R **RESEARCH** - LOOK UP WORDS - CROSS REFERENCES - COMMENTARY

S SUMMARY - SUMMARIZE YOUR FINDINGS-WHAT DOES THE PASSAGE TEACH YOU ABOUT YOUR RELATIONSHIP WITH GOD AND OTHERS

H HOLY SPIRIT - PRAY AND ASK THE HOLY SPIRIT TO SPEAK TO YOU THROUGH THE PASSAGE - WRITE DOWN WHAT YOU HEAR

I INTERNALIZE AND APPLY - HOW DOES THE PASSAGE RELATE TO YOU AND YOUR WALK WITH THE LORD

P PRAY - PRAY THROUGH THE VERSE OR PASSAGE -THANK THE LORD FOR HIS TRUTHS WRITTEN IN THE WORD

READ

Psalm 145:1-7

WORSHIP

Psalm 145:4

Psalm 145:1-7

1 I will extol you, my God and King,

and bless your name forever and ever.

2 Every day I will bless you

land praise your name forever and ever.

3 Great is the LORD, and greatly to be praised,

and his greatness is unsearchable.

4 One generation shall commend your works to another,

and shall declare your mighty acts.

5 On the glorious splendor of your majesty,

and on your wondrous works, I will meditate.

6 They shall speak of the might of your awesome deeds,

and I will declare your greatness.

7 They shall pour forth the fame of your abundant goodness

and shall sing aloud of your righteousness.

Worship Through The Word

W **WRITE THE VERSE** - CIRCLE WORDS TO LOOK UP - HIGHLIGHT

_____

_____

_____

_____

_____

_____

_____

_____

O **OBSERVE** - READ SURROUNDING VERSES - WHO, WHAT, WHEN, WHERE, HOW, WHY

_____

_____

_____

_____

_____

_____

_____

_____

_____

R **RESEARCH** - LOOK UP WORDS - CROSS REFERENCES - COMMENTARY

_____

_____

_____

_____

_____

_____

_____

_____

S **SUMMARY** - SUMMARIZE YOUR FINDINGS-WHAT DOES THE PASSAGE TEACH YOU ABOUT YOUR RELATIONSHIP WITH GOD AND OTHERS

H **HOLY SPIRIT -** PRAY AND ASK THE HOLY SPIRIT TO SPEAK TO YOU THROUGH THE PASSAGE - WRITE DOWN WHAT YOU HEAR

I **INTERNALIZE AND APPLY** - HOW DOES THE PASSAGE RELATE TO YOU AND YOUR WALK WITH THE LORD

P **PRAY** - PRAY THROUGH THE VERSE OR PASSAGE -THANK THE LORD FOR HIS TRUTHS WRITTEN IN THE WORD

READ

Psalm 145:8-13

WORSHIP

Psalm 145:8-9

Psalm 145:8-13

8 The LORD is gracious and merciful,

slow to anger and abounding in steadfast love.

9 The LORD is good to all,

and his mercy is over all that he has made.

10 All your works shall give thanks to you, O LORD,

and all your saints shall bless you!

11 They shall speak of the glory of your kingdom

and tell of your power,

12 to make known to the children of man your mighty deeds,

and the glorious splendor of your kingdom.

13 Your kingdom is an everlasting kingdom,

and your dominion endures throughout all generations.

The LORD is faithful in all his words

and kind in all his works.

Worship Through The Word

W **WRITE THE VERSE** - CIRCLE WORDS TO LOOK UP - HIGHLIGHT

_____
_____
_____
_____
_____
_____
_____
_____

O **OBSERVE** - READ SURROUNDING VERSES - WHO, WHAT, WHEN, WHERE, HOW, WHY

_____
_____
_____
_____
_____
_____
_____
_____

R **RESEARCH** - LOOK UP WORDS - CROSS REFERENCES - COMMENTARY

_____
_____
_____
_____
_____
_____
_____
_____

S SUMMARY - SUMMARIZE YOUR FINDINGS-WHAT DOES THE PASSAGE TEACH YOU ABOUT YOUR RELATIONSHIP WITH GOD AND OTHERS

H HOLY SPIRIT - PRAY AND ASK THE HOLY SPIRIT TO SPEAK TO YOU THROUGH THE PASSAGE - WRITE DOWN WHAT YOU HEAR

I INTERNALIZE AND APPLY - HOW DOES THE PASSAGE RELATE TO YOU AND YOUR WALK WITH THE LORD

P PRAY - PRAY THROUGH THE VERSE OR PASSAGE -THANK THE LORD FOR HIS TRUTHS WRITTEN IN THE WORD

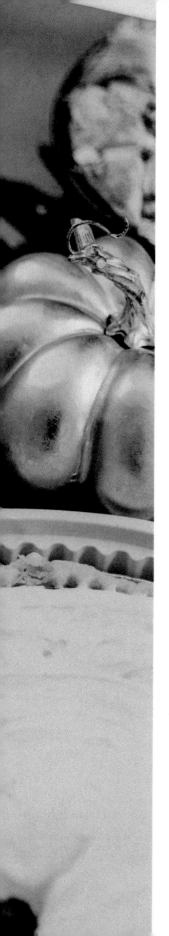

READ
Psalm 145:14-20, Psalm 104:27-28

WORSHIP
Psalm 145:15-16

_____

Psalm 145:14-20

14 The LORD upholds all who are falling
and raises up all who are bowed down.
15 The eyes of all look to you,
and you give them their food in due season.
16 You open your hand;
you satisfy the desire of every living thing.
17 The LORD is righteous in all his ways
and kind in all his works.
18 The LORD is near to all who call on him,
to all who call on him in truth.
19 He fulfills the desire of those who fear him;
he also hears their cry and saves them.
20 The LORD preserves all who love him,
but all the wicked he will destroy.

Psalm 104:27-28

27 These all look to you,
to give them their food in due season.
28 When you give it to them, they gather it up;
when you open your hand,
they are filled with good things.

Worship Through The Word

W   **WRITE THE VERSE** - CIRCLE WORDS TO LOOK UP - HIGHLIGHT

_____
_____
_____
_____
_____
_____
_____

O   **OBSERVE** - READ SURROUNDING VERSES - WHO, WHAT, WHEN, WHERE, HOW, WHY

_____
_____
_____
_____
_____
_____
_____
_____

R   **RESEARCH** - LOOK UP WORDS - CROSS REFERENCES - COMMENTARY

_____
_____
_____
_____
_____
_____
_____

S SUMMARY - SUMMARIZE YOUR FINDINGS-WHAT DOES THE PASSAGE TEACH YOU ABOUT YOUR RELATIONSHIP WITH GOD AND OTHERS

_____

_____

_____

_____

_____

H HOLY SPIRIT - PRAY AND ASK THE HOLY SPIRIT TO SPEAK TO YOU THROUGH THE PASSAGE - WRITE DOWN WHAT YOU HEAR

_____

_____

_____

_____

_____

I INTERNALIZE AND APPLY - HOW DOES THE PASSAGE RELATE TO YOU AND YOUR WALK WITH THE LORD

_____

_____

_____

_____

_____

P PRAY - PRAY THROUGH THE VERSE OR PASSAGE -THANK THE LORD FOR HIS TRUTHS WRITTEN IN THE WORD

_____

_____

_____

_____

_____

READ
Psalm 107:8-9, Psalm 34:10, Psalm 146:7, Luke 1:53

WORSHIP
Psalm 107:9

Psalm 107:8-9

8 Let them thank the LORD for his steadfast love,
for his wondrous works to the children of man!
9 For he satisfies the longing soul,
sand the hungry soul he fills with good things.

Psalm 34:10

10 The young lions suffer want and hunger;
but those who seek the LORD lack no good thing.

Psalm 146:7

7 who executes justice for the oppressed,
who gives food to the hungry.

Luke 1:53

53 he has filled the hungry with good things,
and the rich he has sent away empty.

Worship Through The Word

W **WRITE THE VERSE** - CIRCLE WORDS TO LOOK UP - HIGHLIGHT

_____
_____
_____
_____
_____
_____
_____
_____

O **OBSERVE** - READ SURROUNDING VERSES - WHO, WHAT, WHEN, WHERE, HOW, WHY

_____
_____
_____
_____
_____
_____
_____
_____
_____

R **RESEARCH** - LOOK UP WORDS - CROSS REFERENCES - COMMENTARY

_____
_____
_____
_____
_____
_____
_____
_____

S **SUMMARY** - SUMMARIZE YOUR FINDINGS-WHAT DOES THE PASSAGE TEACH YOU ABOUT YOUR RELATIONSHIP WITH GOD AND OTHERS

_____

_____

_____

_____

H **HOLY SPIRIT** - PRAY AND ASK THE HOLY SPIRIT TO SPEAK TO YOU THROUGH THE PASSAGE - WRITE DOWN WHAT YOU HEAR

_____

_____

_____

_____

I **INTERNALIZE AND APPLY** - HOW DOES THE PASSAGE RELATE TO YOU AND YOUR WALK WITH THE LORD

_____

_____

_____

_____

P **PRAY** - PRAY THROUGH THE VERSE OR PASSAGE -THANK THE LORD FOR HIS TRUTHS WRITTEN IN THE WORD

_____

_____

_____

_____

I give you thanks, O Lord with my whole heart

PSALM 138:1

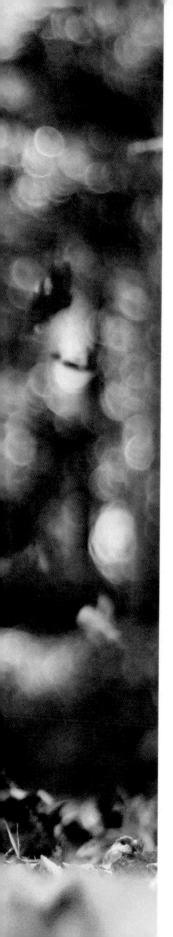

READ

Psalm 106:1-3, 1 John 2:28-29, 1 John 3:7

WORSHIP

1 John 2:29

_____

Psalm 106:1-3

1 Praise the LORD!

Oh give thanks to the LORD, for he is good,

for his steadfast love endures forever!

2 Who can utter the mighty deeds of the LORD,

or declare all his praise?

3 Blessed are they who observe justice,

who do righteousness at all times!

1 John 2:28-29

28 And now, little children, abide in him,

so that when he appears we may have confidence

and not shrink from him in shame at his coming.

29 If you know that he is righteous,

you may be sure that everyone who practices

righteousness has been born of him.

1 John 3:7

7 Little children, let no one deceive you.

Whoever practices righteousness is righteous,

as he is righteous.

Worship Through The Word

W   **WRITE THE VERSE** - CIRCLE WORDS TO LOOK UP - HIGHLIGHT

_____

_____

_____

_____

_____

_____

_____

O   **OBSERVE** - READ SURROUNDING VERSES - WHO, WHAT, WHEN, WHERE, HOW, WHY

_____

_____

_____

_____

_____

_____

_____

R   **RESEARCH** - LOOK UP WORDS - CROSS REFERENCES - COMMENTARY

_____

_____

_____

_____

_____

_____

S SUMMARY - SUMMARIZE YOUR FINDINGS-WHAT DOES THE PASSAGE TEACH YOU ABOUT YOUR RELATIONSHIP WITH GOD AND OTHERS

H HOLY SPIRIT - PRAY AND ASK THE HOLY SPIRIT TO SPEAK TO YOU THROUGH THE PASSAGE - WRITE DOWN WHAT YOU HEAR

I INTERNALIZE AND APPLY - HOW DOES THE PASSAGE RELATE TO YOU AND YOUR WALK WITH THE LORD

P PRAY - PRAY THROUGH THE VERSE OR PASSAGE -THANK THE LORD FOR HIS TRUTHS WRITTEN IN THE WORD

READ
Psalm 107:1-7, Psalm 107:36

WORSHIP
Psalm 107:7

Psalm 107:1-7

1 Oh give thanks to the LORD, for he is good,
for his steadfast love endures forever!
2 Let the redeemed of the LORD say so,
whom he has redeemed from trouble
3 and gathered in from the lands,
from the east and from the west,
from the north and from the south.
4 Some wandered in desert wastes,
finding no way to a city to dwell in;
5 hungry and thirsty,
their soul fainted within them.
6 Then they cried to the LORD in their trouble,
and he delivered them from their distress.
7 He led them by a straight way
till they reached a city to dwell in.

Psalm 107:36

36 And there he lets the hungry dwell,
and they establish a city to live in;

Worship Through The Word

W   **WRITE THE VERSE** - CIRCLE WORDS TO LOOK UP - HIGHLIGHT

O   **OBSERVE** - READ SURROUNDING VERSES - WHO, WHAT, WHEN, WHERE, HOW, WHY

R   **RESEARCH** - LOOK UP WORDS - CROSS REFERENCES - COMMENTARY

S SUMMARY - SUMMARIZE YOUR FINDINGS-WHAT DOES THE PASSAGE TEACH YOU ABOUT YOUR RELATIONSHIP WITH GOD AND OTHERS

H HOLY SPIRIT - PRAY AND ASK THE HOLY SPIRIT TO SPEAK TO YOU THROUGH THE PASSAGE - WRITE DOWN WHAT YOU HEAR

I INTERNALIZE AND APPLY - HOW DOES THE PASSAGE RELATE TO YOU AND YOUR WALK WITH THE LORD

P PRAY - PRAY THROUGH THE VERSE OR PASSAGE -THANK THE LORD FOR HIS TRUTHS WRITTEN IN THE WORD

READ
Psalm 28:6-9, Psalm 3:3-4, Psalm 11:1

WORSHIP
Psalm 28:7

Psalm 28:6-9

6 Blessed be the LORD!
For he has heard the voice of my pleas for mercy.
7 The LORD is my strength and my shield;
in him my heart trusts, and I am helped;
my heart exults,
and with my song I give thanks to him.
8 The LORD is the strength of his people;
he is the saving refuge of his anointed.
9 Oh, save your people and bless your heritage!
Be their shepherd and carry them forever.

Psalm 3:3-4

3 But you, O LORD, are a shield about me,
my glory, and the lifter of my head.
4 I cried aloud to the LORD,
and he answered me from his holy hill.

Psalm 11:1

1 In the LORD I take refuge;
how can you say to my soul,
"Flee like a bird to your mountain,

Worship Through The Word

W   **WRITE THE VERSE** - CIRCLE WORDS TO LOOK UP - HIGHLIGHT

_____

_____

_____

_____

_____

_____

_____

_____

O   **OBSERVE** - READ SURROUNDING VERSES - WHO, WHAT, WHEN, WHERE, HOW, WHY

_____

_____

_____

_____

_____

_____

_____

_____

_____

R   **RESEARCH** - LOOK UP WORDS - CROSS REFERENCES - COMMENTARY

_____

_____

_____

_____

_____

_____

_____

S **SUMMARY** - SUMMARIZE YOUR FINDINGS-WHAT DOES THE PASSAGE TEACH YOU ABOUT YOUR RELATIONSHIP WITH GOD AND OTHERS

_____

_____

_____

_____

_____

H **HOLY SPIRIT -** PRAY AND ASK THE HOLY SPIRIT TO SPEAK TO YOU THROUGH THE PASSAGE - WRITE DOWN WHAT YOU HEAR

_____

_____

_____

_____

_____

I **INTERNALIZE AND APPLY** - HOW DOES THE PASSAGE RELATE TO YOU AND YOUR WALK WITH THE LORD

_____

_____

_____

_____

_____

P **PRAY** - PRAY THROUGH THE VERSE OR PASSAGE -THANK THE LORD FOR HIS TRUTHS WRITTEN IN THE WORD

_____

_____

_____

_____

_____

READ
Psalm 116:12-19

WORSHIP
Psalm 116:17

_____

Psalm 116:12-19

12 What shall I render to the LORD
for all his benefits to me?
13 I will lift up the cup of salvation
and call on the name of the LORD,
14 I will pay my vows to the LORD
in the presence of all his people.
15 Precious in the sight of the LORD
is the death of his saints.
16 O LORD, I am your servant;
I am your servant, the son of your maidservant.
You have loosed my bonds.
17 I will offer to you the sacrifice of thanksgiving
and call on the name of the LORD.
18 I will pay my vows to the LORD
in the presence of all his people,
19 in the courts of the house of the LORD,
in your midst, O Jerusalem.
Praise the LORD!

Worship Through The Word

W   **WRITE THE VERSE** - CIRCLE WORDS TO LOOK UP - HIGHLIGHT

_____

_____

_____

_____

_____

_____

_____

O   **OBSERVE** - READ SURROUNDING VERSES - WHO, WHAT, WHEN, WHERE, HOW, WHY

_____

_____

_____

_____

_____

_____

_____

_____

R   **RESEARCH** - LOOK UP WORDS - CROSS REFERENCES - COMMENTARY

_____

_____

_____

_____

_____

_____

_____

S **SUMMARY** - SUMMARIZE YOUR FINDINGS-WHAT DOES THE PASSAGE TEACH YOU ABOUT YOUR RELATIONSHIP WITH GOD AND OTHERS

_____
_____
_____
_____

H **HOLY SPIRIT -** PRAY AND ASK THE HOLY SPIRIT TO SPEAK TO YOU THROUGH THE PASSAGE - WRITE DOWN WHAT YOU HEAR

_____
_____
_____
_____
_____

I **INTERNALIZE AND APPLY** - HOW DOES THE PASSAGE RELATE TO YOU AND YOUR WALK WITH THE LORD

_____
_____
_____
_____
_____

P **PRAY** - PRAY THROUGH THE VERSE OR PASSAGE -THANK THE LORD FOR HIS TRUTHS WRITTEN IN THE WORD

_____
_____
_____
_____
_____

READ
Psalm 117:1-2, Psalm 103:11-16

WORSHIP
Psalm 103:12

_____

Psalm 117:1-2

1 Praise the LORD, all nations!
Extol him, all peoples!
2 For great is his steadfast love toward us,
and the faithfulness of the LORD endures forever.
Praise the LORD!

Psalm 103:11-16

11 For as high as the heavens are above the earth,
so great is his steadfast love toward those who fear him;
12 as far as the east is from the west,
so far does he remove our transgressions from us.
13 As a father shows compassion to his children,
so the LORD shows compassion to those who fear him.
14 For he knows our frame;*1*
he remembers that we are dust.
15 As for man, his days are like grass;
he flourishes like a flower of the field;
16 for the wind passes over it, and it is gone,
and its place knows it no more.

Worship Through The Word

W   **WRITE THE VERSE** - CIRCLE WORDS TO LOOK UP - HIGHLIGHT

_____

_____

_____

_____

_____

_____

O   **OBSERVE** - READ SURROUNDING VERSES - WHO, WHAT, WHEN, WHERE, HOW, WHY

_____

_____

_____

_____

_____

_____

_____

R   **RESEARCH** - LOOK UP WORDS - CROSS REFERENCES - COMMENTARY

_____

_____

_____

_____

_____

_____

_____

S **SUMMARY** - SUMMARIZE YOUR FINDINGS-WHAT DOES THE PASSAGE TEACH YOU ABOUT YOUR RELATIONSHIP WITH GOD AND OTHERS

_____

_____

_____

_____

H **HOLY SPIRIT -** PRAY AND ASK THE HOLY SPIRIT TO SPEAK TO YOU THROUGH THE PASSAGE - WRITE DOWN WHAT YOU HEAR

_____

_____

_____

_____

I **INTERNALIZE AND APPLY** - HOW DOES THE PASSAGE RELATE TO YOU AND YOUR WALK WITH THE LORD

_____

_____

_____

_____

P **PRAY** - PRAY THROUGH THE VERSE OR PASSAGE -THANK THE LORD FOR HIS TRUTHS WRITTEN IN THE WORD

_____

_____

_____

_____

_____

READ

Psalm 139:1-6

WORSHIP

Psalm 139:1

_____

Psalm 139:1-6

1 O LORD, you have searched me and known me!
2 You know when I sit down and when I rise up;
you discern my thoughts from afar.
3 You search out my path and my lying down
and are acquainted with all my ways.
4 Even before a word is on my tongue,
behold, O LORD, you know it altogether.
5 You *t*hem me in, behind and before,
and lay your hand upon me.
6 Such knowledge is too wonderful for me;
it is high; I cannot attain it.

W   **WRITE THE VERSE** - CIRCLE WORDS TO LOOK UP - HIGHLIGHT

_____

_____

_____

_____

_____

_____

_____

_____

O   **OBSERVE** - READ SURROUNDING VERSES - WHO, WHAT, WHEN, WHERE, HOW, WHY

_____

_____

_____

_____

_____

_____

_____

_____

_____

R   **RESEARCH** - LOOK UP WORDS - CROSS REFERENCES - COMMENTARY

_____

_____

_____

_____

_____

_____

_____

_____

S **SUMMARY** - SUMMARIZE YOUR FINDINGS-WHAT DOES THE PASSAGE TEACH YOU ABOUT YOUR RELATIONSHIP WITH GOD AND OTHERS

_____

_____

_____

_____

H **HOLY SPIRIT -** PRAY AND ASK THE HOLY SPIRIT TO SPEAK TO YOU THROUGH THE PASSAGE - WRITE DOWN WHAT YOU HEAR

_____

_____

_____

_____

I **INTERNALIZE AND APPLY** - HOW DOES THE PASSAGE RELATE TO YOU AND YOUR WALK WITH THE LORD

_____

_____

_____

_____

P **PRAY** - PRAY THROUGH THE VERSE OR PASSAGE -THANK THE LORD FOR HIS TRUTHS WRITTEN IN THE WORD

_____

_____

_____

_____

_____

READ
Psalm 119:1–8

WORSHIP
Psalm 119:7

Psalm 119:1-8

1 Blessed are those whose way is blameless,
who walk in the law of the LORD!
2 Blessed are those who keep his testimonies,
who seek him with their whole heart,
3 who also do no wrong,
but walk in his ways!
4 You have commanded your precepts
to be kept diligently.
5 Oh that my ways may be steadfast
in keeping your statutes!
6 Then I shall not be put to shame,
having my eyes fixed on all your commandments.
7 I will praise you with an upright heart,
when I learn your righteous rules.
8 I will keep your statutes;
do not utterly forsake me!

Worship Through The Word

W   **WRITE THE VERSE** - CIRCLE WORDS TO LOOK UP - HIGHLIGHT

_____
_____
_____
_____
_____
_____
_____

O   **OBSERVE** - READ SURROUNDING VERSES - WHO, WHAT, WHEN, WHERE, HOW, WHY

_____
_____
_____
_____
_____
_____
_____
_____
_____

R   **RESEARCH** - LOOK UP WORDS - CROSS REFERENCES - COMMENTARY

_____
_____
_____
_____
_____
_____
_____

S SUMMARY - SUMMARIZE YOUR FINDINGS-WHAT DOES THE PASSAGE TEACH YOU ABOUT YOUR RELATIONSHIP WITH GOD AND OTHERS

_____
_____
_____
_____

H HOLY SPIRIT - PRAY AND ASK THE HOLY SPIRIT TO SPEAK TO YOU THROUGH THE PASSAGE - WRITE DOWN WHAT YOU HEAR

_____
_____
_____
_____

I INTERNALIZE AND APPLY - HOW DOES THE PASSAGE RELATE TO YOU AND YOUR WALK WITH THE LORD

_____
_____
_____
_____

P PRAY - PRAY THROUGH THE VERSE OR PASSAGE -THANK THE LORD FOR HIS TRUTHS WRITTEN IN THE WORD

_____
_____
_____
_____

Remember the wondrous works that he has done, his miracles, and the judgments he uttered

PSALM 105:5

READ
Psalm 136:1-9

WORSHIP
136:2

———————

Psalm 136:1-9

1 Give thanks to the LORD, for he is good,

for his steadfast love endures forever.

2 Give thanks to the God of gods,

for his steadfast love endures forever.

3 Give thanks to the Lord of lords,

for his steadfast love endures forever;

4 to him who alone does great wonders,

for his steadfast love endures forever;

5 to him who by understanding made the heavens,

for his steadfast love endures forever;

6 to him who spread out the earth above the waters,

for his steadfast love endures forever;

7 to him who made the great lights,

for his steadfast love endures forever;

8 the sun to rule over the day,

for his steadfast love endures forever;

9 the moon and stars to rule over the night,

for his steadfast love endures forever;

W WRITE THE VERSE - CIRCLE WORDS TO LOOK UP - HIGHLIGHT

O OBSERVE - READ SURROUNDING VERSES - WHO, WHAT, WHEN, WHERE, HOW, WHY

R RESEARCH - LOOK UP WORDS - CROSS REFERENCES - COMMENTARY

S SUMMARY - SUMMARIZE YOUR FINDINGS-WHAT DOES THE PASSAGE TEACH YOU ABOUT YOUR RELATIONSHIP WITH GOD AND OTHERS

H HOLY SPIRIT - PRAY AND ASK THE HOLY SPIRIT TO SPEAK TO YOU THROUGH THE PASSAGE - WRITE DOWN WHAT YOU HEAR

I INTERNALIZE AND APPLY - HOW DOES THE PASSAGE RELATE TO YOU AND YOUR WALK WITH THE LORD

P PRAY - PRAY THROUGH THE VERSE OR PASSAGE -THANK THE LORD FOR HIS TRUTHS WRITTEN IN THE WORD

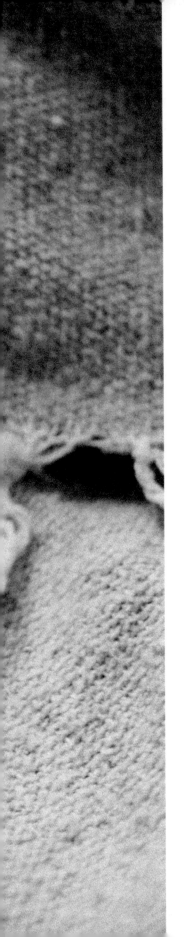

READ

Psalm 136:23-26

WORSHIP

Psalm 136:23

Psalm 136:23-26

23 It is he who remembered us in our low estate,

for his steadfast love endures forever;

24 and rescued us from our foes,

for his steadfast love endures forever;

25 he who gives food to all flesh,

for his steadfast love endures forever.

26 Give thanks to the God of heaven,

for his steadfast love endures forever.

Worship Through The Word

W   **WRITE THE VERSE** - CIRCLE WORDS TO LOOK UP - HIGHLIGHT

_____

_____

_____

_____

_____

_____

O   **OBSERVE** - READ SURROUNDING VERSES - WHO, WHAT, WHEN, WHERE, HOW, WHY

_____

_____

_____

_____

_____

_____

R   **RESEARCH** - LOOK UP WORDS - CROSS REFERENCES - COMMENTARY

_____

_____

_____

_____

_____

_____

S SUMMARY - SUMMARIZE YOUR FINDINGS-WHAT DOES THE PASSAGE TEACH YOU ABOUT YOUR RELATIONSHIP WITH GOD AND OTHERS

H HOLY SPIRIT - PRAY AND ASK THE HOLY SPIRIT TO SPEAK TO YOU THROUGH THE PASSAGE - WRITE DOWN WHAT YOU HEAR

I INTERNALIZE AND APPLY - HOW DOES THE PASSAGE RELATE TO YOU AND YOUR WALK WITH THE LORD

P PRAY - PRAY THROUGH THE VERSE OR PASSAGE -THANK THE LORD FOR HIS TRUTHS WRITTEN IN THE WORD

READ
Psalm 50:14-15 , Psalm 50: 23

WORSHIP
Psalm 50:23

———————————

Psalm 50:14-15

14 Offer to God a sacrifice of thanksgiving,
and perform your vows to the Most High,
15 and call upon me in the day of trouble;
I will deliver you, and you shall glorify me."

Psalm 50:23

23 The one who offers thanksgiving as his sacrifice glorifies me;
to one who orders his way rightly
I will show the salvation of God!"

Worship Through The Word

W   **WRITE THE VERSE** - CIRCLE WORDS TO LOOK UP - HIGHLIGHT

_____

_____

_____

_____

_____

_____

_____

O   **OBSERVE** - READ SURROUNDING VERSES - WHO, WHAT, WHEN, WHERE, HOW, WHY

_____

_____

_____

_____

_____

_____

_____

_____

R   **RESEARCH** - LOOK UP WORDS - CROSS REFERENCES - COMMENTARY

_____

_____

_____

_____

_____

_____

_____

S SUMMARY - SUMMARIZE YOUR FINDINGS-WHAT DOES THE PASSAGE TEACH YOU ABOUT YOUR RELATIONSHIP WITH GOD AND OTHERS

H HOLY SPIRIT - PRAY AND ASK THE HOLY SPIRIT TO SPEAK TO YOU THROUGH THE PASSAGE - WRITE DOWN WHAT YOU HEAR

I INTERNALIZE AND APPLY - HOW DOES THE PASSAGE RELATE TO YOU AND YOUR WALK WITH THE LORD

P PRAY - PRAY THROUGH THE VERSE OR PASSAGE -THANK THE LORD FOR HIS TRUTHS WRITTEN IN THE WORD

READ
Psalm 92:1-5

WORSHIP
Psalm 92:4

_____

Psalm 92:1-5

1 It is good to give thanks to the LORD,
to sing praises to your name, O Most High;
2 to declare your steadfast love in the morning,
and your faithfulness by night,
3 to the music of the lute and the harp,
to the melody of the lyre.
4 For you, O LORD, have made me glad by your work;
at the works of your hands I sing for joy.
5 How great are your works, O LORD!
Your thoughts are very deep!

Worship Through The Word

W **WRITE THE VERSE** - CIRCLE WORDS TO LOOK UP - HIGHLIGHT

_____
_____
_____
_____
_____
_____
_____
_____

O **OBSERVE** - READ SURROUNDING VERSES - WHO, WHAT, WHEN, WHERE, HOW, WHY

_____
_____
_____
_____
_____
_____
_____
_____

R **RESEARCH** - LOOK UP WORDS - CROSS REFERENCES - COMMENTARY

_____
_____
_____
_____
_____
_____
_____

S SUMMARY - SUMMARIZE YOUR FINDINGS-WHAT DOES THE PASSAGE TEACH YOU ABOUT YOUR RELATIONSHIP WITH GOD AND OTHERS

H HOLY SPIRIT - PRAY AND ASK THE HOLY SPIRIT TO SPEAK TO YOU THROUGH THE PASSAGE - WRITE DOWN WHAT YOU HEAR

I INTERNALIZE AND APPLY - HOW DOES THE PASSAGE RELATE TO YOU AND YOUR WALK WITH THE LORD

P PRAY - PRAY THROUGH THE VERSE OR PASSAGE -THANK THE LORD FOR HIS TRUTHS WRITTEN IN THE WORD

READ

Psalm 96:1-13

WORSHIP

Psalm 96:9

_____

Psalm 96:1-13

1 Oh sing to the LORD a new song;

sing to the LORD, all the earth!

2 Sing to the LORD, bless his name;

tell of his salvation from day to day.

3 Declare his glory among the nations,

his marvelous works among all the peoples!

4 For great is the LORD, and greatly to be praised;

he is to be feared above fall gods.

5 For all the gods of the peoples are worthless idols,

but the LORD made the heavens.

6 Splendor and majesty are before him;

strength and beauty are in his sanctuary.

7 Ascribe to the LORD, O families of the peoples,

ascribe to the LORD glory and strength!

8 Ascribe to the LORD the glory due his name;

bring an offering, and come into his courts!

9 Worship the LORD in the splendor of holiness;

tremble before him, all the earth!

10 Say among the nations, "The LORD reigns!

Yes, the world is established; it shall never be moved;

he will judge the peoples with equity."

11 Let the heavens be glad, and let the earth rejoice;

let the sea roar, and all that fills it;

12 let the field exult, and everything in it!

Then shall all the trees of the forest sing for joy

13 before the LORD, for he comes,

for he comes to judge the earth.

He will judge the world in righteousness,

and the peoples in his faithfulness.

Worship Through The Word

W   **WRITE THE VERSE** - CIRCLE WORDS TO LOOK UP - HIGHLIGHT

_____
_____
_____
_____
_____
_____
_____
_____

O   **OBSERVE** - READ SURROUNDING VERSES - WHO, WHAT, WHEN, WHERE, HOW, WHY

_____
_____
_____
_____
_____
_____
_____
_____

R   **RESEARCH** - LOOK UP WORDS - CROSS REFERENCES - COMMENTARY

_____
_____
_____
_____
_____
_____
_____

S SUMMARY - SUMMARIZE YOUR FINDINGS-WHAT DOES THE PASSAGE TEACH YOU ABOUT YOUR RELATIONSHIP WITH GOD AND OTHERS

H HOLY SPIRIT - PRAY AND ASK THE HOLY SPIRIT TO SPEAK TO YOU THROUGH THE PASSAGE - WRITE DOWN WHAT YOU HEAR

I INTERNALIZE AND APPLY - HOW DOES THE PASSAGE RELATE TO YOU AND YOUR WALK WITH THE LORD

P PRAY - PRAY THROUGH THE VERSE OR PASSAGE -THANK THE LORD FOR HIS TRUTHS WRITTEN IN THE WORD

READ
Psalm 103:1-9

WORSHIP
Psalm 103:8

Psalm 103:1-9

1 Bless the LORD, O my soul,
and all that is within me,
bless his holy name!
2 Bless the LORD, O my soul,
and forget not all his benefits,
3 who forgives all your iniquity,
who heals all your diseases,
4 who redeems your life from the pit,
who crowns you with steadfast love and mercy,
5 who satisfies you with good
so that your youth is renewed like the eagle's.
6 The LORD works righteousness
and justice for all who are oppressed.
7 He made known his ways to Moses,
his acts to the people of Israel.
8 The LORD is merciful and gracious,
slow to anger and abounding in steadfast love.
9 He will not always chide,
nor will he keep his anger forever.

Worship Through The Word

W   **WRITE THE VERSE** - CIRCLE WORDS TO LOOK UP - HIGHLIGHT

_____
_____
_____
_____
_____
_____
_____
_____

O   **OBSERVE** - READ SURROUNDING VERSES - WHO, WHAT, WHEN, WHERE, HOW, WHY

_____
_____
_____
_____
_____
_____
_____
_____

R   **RESEARCH** - LOOK UP WORDS - CROSS REFERENCES - COMMENTARY

_____
_____
_____
_____
_____
_____
_____

S **SUMMARY** - SUMMARIZE YOUR FINDINGS-WHAT DOES THE PASSAGE TEACH YOU ABOUT YOUR RELATIONSHIP WITH GOD AND OTHERS

_____

_____

_____

_____

H **HOLY SPIRIT -** PRAY AND ASK THE HOLY SPIRIT TO SPEAK TO YOU THROUGH THE PASSAGE - WRITE DOWN WHAT YOU HEAR

_____

_____

_____

_____

I **INTERNALIZE AND APPLY** - HOW DOES THE PASSAGE RELATE TO YOU AND YOUR WALK WITH THE LORD

_____

_____

_____

_____

P **PRAY** - PRAY THROUGH THE VERSE OR PASSAGE -THANK THE LORD FOR HIS TRUTHS WRITTEN IN THE WORD

_____

_____

_____

_____

READ

Psalm 105:1-5

WORSHIP

Psalm 105:4

Psalm 105:1-5

1 Oh give thanks to the LORD; call upon his name;
make known his deeds among the peoples!
2 Sing to him, sing praises to him;
tell of all his wondrous works!
3 Glory in his holy name;
let the hearts of those who seek the LORD rejoice!
4 Seek the LORD and his strength;
seek his presence continually!
5 Remember the wondrous works that he has done,
his miracles, and the judgments he uttered,

Worship Through The Word

W   **WRITE THE VERSE** - CIRCLE WORDS TO LOOK UP - HIGHLIGHT

_____

_____

_____

_____

_____

_____

_____

O   **OBSERVE** - READ SURROUNDING VERSES - WHO, WHAT, WHEN, WHERE, HOW, WHY

_____

_____

_____

_____

_____

_____

_____

_____

R   **RESEARCH** - LOOK UP WORDS - CROSS REFERENCES - COMMENTARY

_____

_____

_____

_____

_____

_____

_____

_____

S **SUMMARY** - SUMMARIZE YOUR FINDINGS-WHAT DOES THE PASSAGE TEACH YOU ABOUT YOUR RELATIONSHIP WITH GOD AND OTHERS

H **HOLY SPIRIT** - PRAY AND ASK THE HOLY SPIRIT TO SPEAK TO YOU THROUGH THE PASSAGE - WRITE DOWN WHAT YOU HEAR

I **INTERNALIZE AND APPLY** - HOW DOES THE PASSAGE RELATE TO YOU AND YOUR WALK WITH THE LORD

P **PRAY** - PRAY THROUGH THE VERSE OR PASSAGE -THANK THE LORD FOR HIS TRUTHS WRITTEN IN THE WORD

Made in the USA
Columbia, SC
29 October 2022

70154086R10077